Revelations of
a Hood Chick

From Ghetto Fabulous to Fabulous

KIJANA LETASHA HARRIS

AuthorHouse™
1663 Liberty Drive
Bloomington, IN 47403
www.authorhouse.com
Phone: 1 (800) 839-8640

Published by AuthorHouse   04/09/2015

ISBN: 978-1-5049-0232-8 (sc)
ISBN: 978-1-5049-0231-1 (e)

Print information available on the last page.

Contents

Soldier

I can't count the blessings
You ever been so blessed you forget,
because you think it's owed
So blessed in your life that you grow cold
Well God uses moments of chaos, trials, and
tribulations, to remind us that we need him
The worst kind of child is the one you spoil
and never hold them accountable
God doesn't want weakness on his team
He needs soldiers
A soldier is built,
First, by his uniform
Stripping off all the street clothes,
the clothes of the world
Then replacing that old attire with a new more suitable
uniform, that will set him apart from the rest of the world
A uniform designed to represent
greatness, bravery, and endurance
Second, by his mind
Breaking him away from his former way of thinking
Drilling into his mind the new truths, his
mission, his purpose, his power
Giving him a new mind and a new thought process
Third, severe training
Training of both the mind and the body repeating
the new songs and lessons enduring intense
training with blood, sweat, and tears
Building him for battle, preparing him for war

Getting him so strong he's swifter, wiser,
more prepared than ever before
Sharpening his sword
Training continues daily, with discipline being enforced
Learning how to carry himself properly
in all classes of people
Fourth, the benefits
The soldier reaps all the financial and
social levels to the highest marking
He also has gratitude and self-appreciation from not
giving up and pushing through the transformation
He is now honored by many, hated by few
A soldier of prestige and humility
Every day that soldier is a soldier, living
daily, but ready to be called for war
That is exactly how God builds his disciples
Getting rid of the old clothes and putting on his armor
Transforming our old thoughts to righteous thoughts
Renewing of the mind, body, and spirit
So all of our trials and tribulations
are a part of our training,
Building us up, preparing us for life's constant battles
Each little battle gives us the tools we
will need for the wars to come
When we feel low or defeated
When we feel tired and overwhelmed
When we need strength, backup, or
reminding we call on God

And he replenishes us with exactly
what we need to keep going
So when that trial is over and victory is ours we can
celebrate and rejoice, enjoying the rewards of winning
Living in peace, joy, and harmony,
until the next call for war
That's why it is important to remember your
training and never forget who built you.
Stay Ready

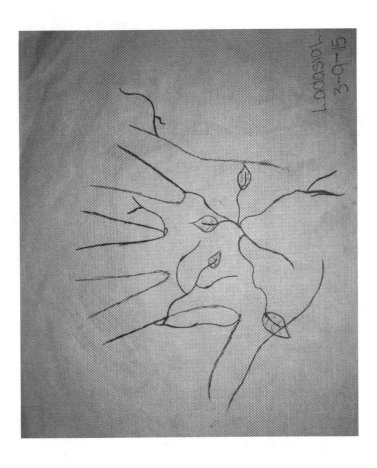

Miracles We Ignore

You think it's redundant that people always say thank God for waking up this morning. Well, the truth is you should. Every day that you have been awakened, you are given a chance to live different, think different, and become better. It took a lot of bad relationships for me to sit down and look at me to see the problem. I have given me to everyone but me. But, God, oh God has given me another chance to love me by waking me up this morning.

I got caught up in the world view of what I need and I got four beautiful children out of it, but I also had to suffer the consequences of my sins. My choices to fornicate, marry unequally yoked, to live a lie, and basically play house with men was all my sin. I can't cry and complain about my lack when I chose not to be patient and wait on the Lord. Know, when we choose people over God, we lose a piece of ourselves. I used so much energy loving everyone but God, I became weak.

I got a rude awakening. I was told by many men they hate me and wish they weren't with me. They would say I was crazy for setting boundaries, sometimes physically fighting me. Telling me I was not worth it. Treating me like a whore, and I accepted it when I stayed. I used to cry, because I thought they loved me. Those words were harsh. It took a piece of me every time I heard them.

With every relationship I received the same message.
At the time, I didn't see the manifestation of the seed
that was planted. With every sinful relationship that
hate seed was watered. Before I could blink, I was
swimming in self-doubt, and hate. I mean they said
"I love you". But their actions matched the harsh
words of hate, more than the sweet acts of love.
I accepted all the disrespect and disregard because
I didn't know my self-worth. See I didn't realize for
twenty four years I was wounding myself, every time
I would lay down with a man that wasn't my husband.
I didn't see the damage of allowing hate to take loves
place. This is a revelation revealed years ago, but finally
understood. Now I see how important every day is.
If I didn't have God's mercy for a new day, I couldn't
learn a new lesson, or have a reinforced revelation.

Lost Pet Syndrome

My definition

Lost Pet Syndrome is a mental condition. A condition, in which, one feels the overwhelming desire to find the low, broken, and lost. Then nurse them back to health with love, encouragement, and all the basic needs of life. Without one's own knowledge, as your nurturing them, you become mentally involved. You want to give them your whole heart. But because they are broken, they are incapable of returning any type of love to you. Actually becoming strong and resenting your efforts in restoration. They now feel so good they look at your help as a weakness and a need for love. That turns them away and causes them to search for a challenge or something different all together. Then they leave you empty and searching for someone else to save. It's like finding a bird with a broken wing. As soon as their healed and able to fly again, they leave without warning, without care; their a bird and are meant to fly, not be caged. A bird, cannot love you back. They are only capable of doing what birds do. Therefore, Lost Pet Syndrome, results in more mourning than rejoicing. The only way to be cured or delivered from Lost Pet Syndrome is to learn how to love and nurture yourself. Get involved with your own personal healing and growth, then the need to be loved will be lessened and a healthy desire to love will develop.

Appetizers for the Soul

Everything you say can and will be used
against you in the hood of law.
Keep your shortcomings to yourself.

They're not where I'm from they're just where I've been.
Another one bites the dust.

Freedom

Finding yourself is not easy
Looking at a victor it may look breezy
But the truth is it's a purposeful act like
waking up early and starting on track
Don't be deceived problems will come
But knowing who you are will bring you to peace
Take time for yourself let your mind be released

Delivery

Delivery
I need to be delivered from me
Delivery
Looking over at you trying to find me
Delivery
I have been held captive by me
I need to break free from my own chains My pains and
my sorrows set me free When I let them be hallowed
But I wanted to hang on like there was no tomorrow
Delivery
I am breaking free from emotional
strains it does not benefit me any
And I reap no gain
No more looking at you trying to find me
Cause I'm over here nowhere you'd be
I can see you and admire you
But I cannot borrow you or troddle you
Because your you and I'm me
Me, as in I need to be delivered from myself
The expectations I have placed on me are God high
Who am I to fly but not without wings, that I have tucked
away and thought I could still sore almost crashing
to the floor Nothing ever being enough from me
I always needed more
Now I've cut the chains from myself
And I see me again ready to conquer all things
And with lesson learned written on my back
Cause it's behind me
Delivery

Lost Heart

By
Shaunice Primes, my beloved 1st born

We walk this world with our hearts wide open,
We wear it on our sleeves, flossing it to the thief's,
We hurt because it gets broken, abused with
a hammer, because it's made out of glass
Then stop and think to ourselves
how long does this pain last
From the day it got stolen it remains broken,
Everyone we chose to give the shattered
pieces to just makes the cuts deeper,
So we remain broken
We become heartless,
Until we meet the one person who instead of
begging for your pieces for their own good,
They give you their pieces to help you heal, Once
you trust, you start to give them the same
Everything fits perfect, snug
And that's how we fall in love

Worthy

I'm worthy
I'm Awesome
I'm beautiful
I'm divine
I'm blessed
I'm highly favored
I'm what God created
I'm more than enough
This is my truths
Do I have work to do
Well of course
Perfection only comes after death
Bit by bit
I get greater
A new woman
In new skin
With a new mind
Built from within
Nothing is lost
It's is all wins
Even when it's sad
Even when it's scary
Even when I'm afraid
It's still victory
How you ask
Well it's not what I've been through that
defines me it's what I have become;
worthy, awesome, divine, blessed, and highly favored
What God has created

Noise

We've all heard it from someone in our lives
You will never make it
You will fail
You will be just like your mother
Your no good
You're not the one
Who do you think you are
I am what the creator says I am
For you are but of the flesh
You cannot tell me lies
I am a world conqueror
I am divine
How you say
Because he who is greater in he
is greater than the world
Therefore your thorns may poke
Your thorns may cause me to bleed
But your thorns will not direct if I succeed
I have been through the trenches of death
And yet I live

With all my faults and all my shortcomings
I still rise
Like the sun from the east to the west
I have to listen to the father of truth not of lies
He said I was weak
But my father called me strong
He said I was a fool
And God gave me a new song
I will not except your words of vile
I choose to stand up
I choose to smile

Appetizers for the Soul

Hateful Words are like bowel movements,
Once you let it out,
It's impossible to put them back in;
If you try you'll have a stanken mess.

Self-Discussion

Hi me, How are you? I'm actually feeling renewed and restored. I have decided to accept the things that I can't change and trust God to change what needs to be changed in me. I found out that I love me so much I may even be over protective. I was doing such a poor job of loving me in the past I had to regroup and remember that I am who God says I am, not the world. I found out that I no longer need love from a man, Gods love is sufficient. Do you know what that means? That I am no longer bound as a slave of wanting to be accepted or loved; accepting abuse and disrespectful actions from men. I am worth so much more than that. I'm sitting there mad at the world when the reality is, I was neglecting me. It's easy to get confused and think you have to play wife, savior, and all those other roles. I am done looking for it, expecting it, and trying it. Forget it. That may seem harsh, but I just don't think I'm made to go through the motions. Been there done that and they all fail. I ain't wasting another moment of my life thinking about another fool. I threw in the towel of try and I'm doing me. I will be free for life, never again will I go back to that slave mentality. I'm awesome; too good to settle. I was crazy insane, for real doing the same thing time after time expecting different results. I'm not going to sell my soul for lust.

Love is brought by God and they don't even know him.
Lol! I'm 36 now but it took me to move to Houston and
not have a friend or job distracting me. Straight focused,
something is clearly wrong. Wow. But, I am ok now that
I see, and I am moving forward again, not taking any
baggage with me. I am free you hear, I'm not married;
I'm not bound by God

Appetizers for the Soul

Put on your full armor of God
It's a battlefield of the mind
We know what's real,
the devil wants us to see and accept lies
Run to the truth and be set free
Even, if that means being alone

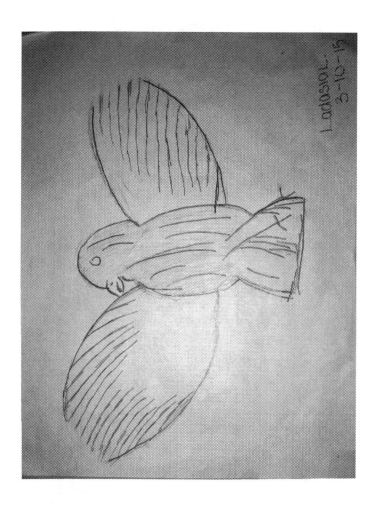

Free

I can walk away
I know I gave all of me I was good to you
Just because we didn't click doesn't
make me feel so sick
I wanted to fall deep in love with you
but you held me at a distance
Suppose it was good for me
because
When you left it didn't make a difference
Sometimes being alone is a gift so strong
We hate to see it but sometimes it needs to come along
I'm free
It feels good not to be judged or treated wrong
It feels good to sleep at night and
not worry anything is wrong
It feels good to not have the pressure of not
getting it right or being good enough
It feels good being free

Inner Thoughts of Hood Esteem

No one defines who or what you are. You're made
you, be you. Do not waste your life living out
what someone else's idea of you should be. Live
exactly how you want, just be ready to handle the
consequences of your choices. Nobody is perfect,
so who can judge you. Live your identity and let
them live theirs. You're beautiful when you are you.

Let's Not Forget the Children

You first raising you was easy until you grew up then I
couldn't tell you my version you had to hear the world's
My safety net gone
My protector radar shot down
Its what they say now
Even your father had something
to say and wasn't around
But you have always been a reflection
of what God saw good in me
He brought you to me to show how great I could be
Your birth was an inspiration of maturity
Changing some things in me
Getting me baptized
Giving my heart to God
You gave me hope
My first child to see you walk
With each step I mastered going farther
You were my first gift from God
You were a reflection of what good lied in me
My second child dear love of my life
my expression of frustration
Not able to express myself on a level of
understanding you are the voice that will
be heard by my hands I spoke,
I taught a lot of well lessons, well some unnecessary
and you showed me what pain feels like and
the inner me who refuses to get better
Without cause they say go right you go left, my stubborn
spirit always hated authority couldn't nobody tell me,

Well your life caused my life to seek help and get
counseling because of you I saw what I was, was wrong
You are my divine lesson of hurt struggle and yes over
coming of those things that held me from my growth
You a reflection of me a true gift to see you in the
mirror learning how to love yourself as I did alone
Now with you, we are a team
I am not complete without the hard truth you showed
me about me, my love my fire my strength
My inner child forever birthed third,
It was a hard few years to swallow but
you're the reason I can smile,
My reflection from God of what it's like to live
without worry forever being happy knowing
no one can hurt you even if they try
Your tears like raindrops when they fall
they bloom any sadness in me
Your birth took away giving me a soul full of
play I look at you and see the freedom God
promised me the peace I cried for all in you
You inspire me to not go crazy the love you
give silently is louder than lighting
I love you with my whole soul and I thank God
for trusting me with something so precious,
I know I don't deserve you, but you're for
me to see how to stay in my heart.
My last I prayed for you to be and help your brother
My heart cried with joy when God
blessed me with another boy

I knew the King of Kings heard my fear,
I didn't want to go without help and I knew if
God sent you, you would be mine forever,
Anger demanding your soul
Your reflection taught me self-control
You are what I was loud fussy
controlled by my environment
Now I can look and see the revelation the
purpose is to show me how to be graceful
meek in spirit submitting to the will of God
I Am an angel who can feel the pain you feel
it too because you are me and I am you
I know the burn in your head blinds your eyes and
your thoughts become dark, but you have shown me
how to defeat the enemy with a smile on my face
no fear from you, you gave me understanding
I know now what love feels like looks
like it is you and all of you are me.
I love myself better because of you.

My House
A Reflection of Me

I don't think that people are capable of change.
One might say change is necessary to get from
one level to the next. But to me people are
comfortable at their levels. Unless a tragic situation
occurs and it is inevitable that a change be made,
change will not happen. Yes, I have changed,
but my old me sits their taunting me to get out.
It takes an inner strength to keep it with in.
I have been through many trials, I have many still
to go. Can I be prepared to go through them and
come out sane? Every person has demons to
overcome. I have my own, but I am a rare breed.
I know this to be true because when I sit in the
house of God it is empty. For fear of success
holds people back from changing for the better.
My house is dirty. I need to clean it out. My closets
are full of skeletons. My couches pressed down from
weight. My bed dirty from fluids. I need to vacuum my
floors pick up the debris from me and my companies'
shoes. The stains in my carpet stand out. I need to
steam clean my floors. My kitchen stove is dirty, my
food is bitter. My mirrors are dim from the dust, so
my reflection is not clear. I need to clean my inner
me in order to be free and live. I need to throw away
the trash and purchase a new picture. My soul is at
stake. There is no way I can get to heaven like this.

There is a lot of neglect in my house. God save me from myself, because I have become comfortable with less. I have a cup filled to the minimum. What kind of role model am I for my kids? Deliver me from my flesh and let me see the reflection of my soul clear.

Fruitless

The Bible teaches you can tell a tree by the fruit it bears. That means if it's an orange tree it should have oranges, an apple tree should have apples and so on. So I'm going to, translate it to hoodology. If a person is all that they claim to be, it should be evidence of that. So as a Hood chick raised with low expectations, I would accept a fruitless tree. I would look at the empty branches and see the tree for what it could be, instead of what it is. As a woman now who knows better, if the tree ain't got no fruit, it ain't sitting in good soil. That tree is damaged, and will wither away in the elements of what it could have been. It will suck the life out of the surrounding vegetation, and because it's dead it has no love. It does not bloom or cherish nurturing. It is dying and anything that connects with the roots of that fruitless tree will die too. So if you see what looks like a tree, that could produce good fruit, but doesn't have any, run. Go find you a tree that already has bloomed and the fruit is consistently reproducing every season. When you find that, you have found the one. Until then pray for that empty tree, but don't waste a drop of water or soil trying to save it. It's already dead.

Loving

I'm complicated; according to the world I'm strange.
The reality is God loves me with all my flaws. I'm
not religious, so I don't have rules set up to fail.
I'm a believer, and I believe that no matter where we
fall short God is there to cover the distance. People
judge you if you say you're a believer because you
cuss, drink, or any other "sin". But that's okay, because
there not the one who makes your life decisions.
I'm not perfect and don't claim to be.
What I am, is true to myself and I
am loving me some me!

Random Fussing

If I read one more self-help book, I will scream. All the reading in the world can't help me. How can I still be broke after all this education and self-help guides? I am truly blessed and highly favored. Yet I'm barely living check to check. I have been struggling to pay my bills, to feed my children, to getting out of the bed. It takes me twenty minutes to convince myself every day to get up and go to work. I lay there drowning in my own misery, reaching deep inside of me to find a reason to rise. I think about bills, and that sinks me deeper into my low budget pillow top mattress. I need to get new beds for my children. My oldest daughter has been bed-less since we moved to Texas. She's been sleeping on the floor, or she'll make a pallet with the couch pillows. My son Jaylon makes me smile when I think about him. He'll hold is head up so high that if he was standing he'd fall over. Luckily his head is small. Because his neck is weak and it would be even more challenging for him to see the world around him. My Jaylon, wow I just smile when I say his name. He is the cutest disabled child I know. Well, there is this one girl; she has a disabled son too. His face is deformed and due to all the brain surgery he has a lot of scares. But, he is somehow the most adorable. He speaks so well like he has been here before as a scholar of some sort. Well I guess my other two kids won't move unless I do. So let me get them up and off to school. That's what I go through every day I have to come to this slave driving job.

The spill they gave me to convince me to work here was good. Maybe, too good to be true. No lunches, no breaks, no errors; efficiency perfection performance. What could you have done differently they ask... Not came. Grrrr. But, I guess it is all part of God's divine plan.

Faith keeps me in the game. I talk to God often, me mumbling, groaning, and crying usually is our conversation. But I give him honor, because he always shows up right on time. I moved to Houston to live. I go outside more now than in Omaha, so I guess it's a start. Omaha repressed me. I mean, I lost faith in people and trust was nonexistent. There are a lot of selfish people in the world, and I know most of them. From family to friends, you can't rely on anyone there. I have been exposed to hell, almost lived there. But as usual God saved me from me. I try not to complain a lot, so I don't speak to people much. Until I learn how to speak good and not evil I need silence. My life is a bitter sweet roller coaster and I'm in for the long haul. I can't begin to explain my inner thoughts out loud, so I keep drifting off into my head. Let's just say my head is heavy, and my neck is tired. I'm tired of a lot of things, so we're do I start. Well the battlefield of the mind is real. I'm constantly trying different ways to survive, but my final result is always prayer. I wonder why prayer isn't my first choice. It would make my life so much easier to just let go and let God.

Knowledge

There has been many nights I have waited alone wondering where is my man. Relationships for me have all been disappointing and I believe I am a poor judge of character. Or maybe I can see so well with an anointed gift, I see in them what they can't see in themselves. Boring, same ol' pattern, end up broken and cheated. All along I had the power to change the cycle; I just didn't know where to begin.

I loved and lost early. I learned at a vulnerable stage in life not to trust people. I learned that people are selfish hateful beings and could care less about being righteous. For some odd reason, I couldn't adapt that mind frame. No matter how angry or hurt I'd become, I never could master hate.

I suppose I'm different, but being different causes a lot of confusion and chaos. It's like talking to someone of another tongue who has never heard your language before. It's like talking to a brick wall and then running your head into over and over again until the pain leaves and the hurt is normal. Losing the living hurts me more than losing the dead.

I am not sure if that is normal or strange, but I know my kind is rare. When I meet people and I'm attracted to them I lean in to get to know them better. I chose only to see the good. Bad can be jumping out of them like lice in a infested head, and I wouldn't flinch. I'm so strong, it's weak. I'm so strong that I can love someone until I am physically exasperated and still try to love them. I'm so weak that I'm willing to love that hard to people who don't reciprocate it back. I neglect loving the ones who matter the most, me and my children.

I've decided though, that I was going to start paying attention to the signs and standing up for my mind. I've allowed too many bad people too much power. I'm releasing it now, and taking it back. I'm no longer me, I'm Queen me. That means I demand more of me to me. Anyone who entertains the idea of my presence, will earn, respect, and value it. I will no longer accept, mediocre.

Loving Me

Words have power choose them wisely. What is said from the mouth comes from the heart. So think before you speak. If I've been told I'm insecure weak not of good value bad mother dirty dumb crazy old fashioned negative and a slew of other insults that is poison. God has told me I was virtuous a Queen a renewed and restored soul full of love joy and wisdom, who do I listen to? The father of lies or of truth? Love does not hate me, men hate me because I am love. I haven't done anything wrong to any of them except love them. Now I have questioned their faith fullness because as colds present symptoms, so does cheating and lack of love. Love doesn't have reciprocated factors, it is unconditional; but since it is one way I'll let go of the hope of it with you and love through God. I'm done being the only one who loves with action and words. They say hateful things show me hateful ways and say I'm insecure or crazy for questioning the validity of the words. Love is an action word. Speak hate to me and treat me like a non-factor, I do not love me if I accept it.

Trust

Trust is a four letter word
I know you've heard that before
I can't put anything past anyone anymore
I think there is a lot to say about the mind
It can trick you into believing the best or the worst
I have to close my eyes and pray that only
thoughts from God let me think
Only voices from God let me follow
If I listened to my thoughts I would be dead
You have to be careful of the voices in your head
They creep up on you yelling and quarreling
It's quite only when your mourning
See if you recognize they mean you no good
You'd be rejoicing instead from the results of your head

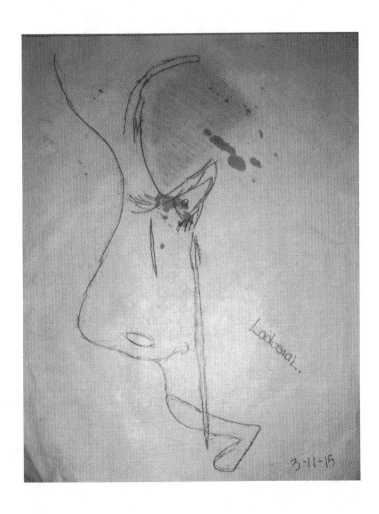

So I Thought

So I said I love you
I thought you were the man I wanted
With harsh words demonstrating your character
With cold hands holding me close
I pull back and see who you are
Now I'm not sure if you're the one
I was convinced before I had to have you
I remember thinking you were all I had been looking for
Even with your efforts of being kind
I feel still in the back of my mind I don't know if I want you
Your critical behavior has caused me to see you with open eyes
I see your ambitious motivation
I see your focus and determination
I force myself to participate in your joy
I make myself available to hear your ploy
All along I'm rethinking my desire for you
You purposely put out my fire I desired your touch your kiss your attention
But now I don't know if your him
I find myself thinking I'm wasting my time
I could be with someone else
I could be someone else
I'm stuck between is it true or is it all in my head
Your words show no attempt to conquer me
Your actions show all attempts to limit me
We Both Like flying
We both desire understanding
We both want to be heard

We both can't see each other as the one
Through discussion I received this message
Which caused my eyes to wonder selfishly I began to
seek out other options
My eyes burning with the flame of passion gives off the
scent of desire resulting in the sniffing of new comers
begging to taste the very flower you refuse to touch how
can I hold on and not give the sip when my loins burn for
the groping and pulling and gushing
I have to be strong and deny myself while I wait for you
to open up and reciprocate the love passion and fire will
it be worth it

Menstrual

Monthly you show up raging with confusion
The swelling, the sharp tear through the flesh
The pulsing and grinding of the muscles
radiating from the height of a small tower to the steps of
the hallowed ground
I suffer you showing up
I know when it's coming the twisting and pulsing that you
bring with you nauseated the belly broken the head as it
falls to the sound of every voice the relentless irritation of
the surrounding thoughts echo for seven days you play
control can't get in a comfortable position no rest in my
own skin misery your pattern changes sometimes more
harsh than others I haven't quite figured out how to calm
you so I prepare every 28 days for your arrival I love to
see you come to know there's no life coming forth
But I love to see you go from the days of my life you take
away

I Found Her

Looking so deep inside of me
I find the tools that have always been there
The skills that kept me prepared
The faith that built me up
The light that guided me
Brightened the inside of me
I knew her once
Now know her again
Joy is here
Standing novation from the peace
Standing novation from the prosperity
All of me is awesome
Divinely made in his image
A reflection of remarkable makings
Transformed from dirt to life
From rib to woman
I am a Queen by right
Purple robe standing high above
Looking to the crowd
I will not follow
I will lead

Healed

The hurt from my past can't last
I see the death of it coming soon
Who knew when it would see its doom
I didn't even know I was affected
Until I seen the trail it projected
Lost love hateful Words inability to love
All symptoms of pain held on
All indications I hadn't moved on
I didn't see it in my mind
It was hidden deep so I couldn't find
A remarkable man showed me his strength
I lost him too because I built a fence
So much pain I held on to he could see it but I didn't think
it was true
I thought I was fine living divine
But then I saw it was still deep inside
It wasn't until he yelled he hated me
Something all men say when their dating me.
I thought it was them all just full of hate
But it was me all along I closed the gate
Only so close could they get in me
I focused on school and work and neglected me
I drank a lot a did random thangs but this was all reflection
of pain
But God sent me someone I actually feared enough to
listen too.
He was towering over me in height big and strong but I
would still fight

Even though his words were harsh
They woke up the fact I was living in the dark
I was angry with him for the things he said in my mind he
was evil and better off dead
But my reality hit while praying one day
That I was full of fear and had bad words to say
Watch my tongue and control it well fear nothing but God
and I'll do well
Later that night I watched a movie
Call me crazy and then it came to me
I have PTSD from all the pain
But there is hope for me to once again be sane

Hater

Go from here you're not wanted
Showing up in my life
Crashing my party
Expecting me to accept anything
Get from here with your shouting
your negative attitude
Hating my swag, I'm fly and you mad
Get from here with your frowned face
Judging me all in my face
I hear your whispers of doubt your double tongue
But you can't touch me
You see God has already won
Run doubt
Bounce fear
Die insecurity
I'm good without you
Say what you want about me
Watch me do it
Hater

Fearless

I'm a beast out here
You didn't want me to unleash the power
So you pressed your foot on my collar
Get those shackles off of me
I can't be defeated failure has come and went I'm still standing,
What you say weeble wobble but I don't fall down
No more tears he says no more pain
I'm riding with soldiers is that so strange
I'm not the typical soft spoken voice nor am I the loud
need all the attention from the crowd
I'm the laughter
The beast that rages only when there's war otherwise
smiling given the world more
You don't want to test me with your games I'm a beast out
here and ready for pain
You can't hold me my enemies have no ground, I was
against myself with you but now I'm found
I'm a beast out here go on settle down
You don't want to get me started my prayer game is fierce
I got Jesus on my team
You don't want none of this
I'm a God made woman come with your A game
If you don't you'll leave weakened and full of shame
No I don't think I'm tough I'm not built by Ford Truck
I'm built by God that makes me Lord tough
I don't have to be mad at you
But I will pray for you
If you would of only knew
The beast in me is truth

Song

When I hear your song
I sway
My body can't hold still shifting from left to right my steps
become a pattern going to the beat of your song
Spinning in circles arching my back bending my knees
my arms going left to right, right to left the bass vibrations
tingling my bones my ears pulsing with the chimes I rise
My neck slithering snake like motions as I sip my potion
I weaken by your song
Eyes closed mind seeing me in your TV can't get you out
of my head feeling the freedom of your song instead

Awakening

How sickening the mind can be
Hidden deep inside I sought me
For years it's been hidden and I couldn't see
Why didn't I look sooner inside of me
I was looking high
I looked low
Never dawned on me at all it was my flow
I didn't pay attention to my own words
One day I looked and it was my voice I heard
I'm tripping over what
Sad because of who
Charity is good but it starts with me
Forgiveness is needed but it starts with me.
Let Go
I thought I did
But sick was disguised with real and hid
Glasses on, I can see it wasn't them doing me wrong it
was me
Where do I start
First with a smile
That I finally got it even if it took a while

Appetizers for the Soul

Thought for the day
If I had no toes, I could not wear flip flops.
It's the little things we take for granted.
Life is short,
Run barefoot

Appetizers for the Soul

Brunch
Liars tend to have esteem issues
Evil people do not love themselves,
therefore, cannot give love
Men really do not think like women
Women, we may think a little bit too much
Some women don't think at all...

Appetizers for the Soul

"Helpful snacks"
Relationships are like a spades game
Ladies, keep one and a possible.

Trust really is on a scale.
Everyone starts off at 99%. Never give
100% to anyone. You can maintain points
or lose them based off of your actions.
Men...
Words don't count unless you speak what you show.

God Sees My Tears

So this morning I woke up and did my little routine and God showed me he sees my tears. First, I read my daily devotional which was titled "Fear has no place". It ministered to my spirit about being courageous like Mary (mother of Jesus). It spoke on how God had asked her to be Jesus mother and depended on her to follow his word. Even though she went through hard times, Mary still did it. Because of her obedience following through, despite her fear, she saved the world. Then I went to my Bible and it started skipping pages; so I trusted it was God taking me to the word I needed to hear. It was about the tongue and how it's a small member but very powerful. It spoke how the ore of a ship or the bit in a horse's mouth was also small, but it did big things, such as stop a horse or directs a ship. My lesson was to follow God's instructions and tame my tongue. It spoke on how a well cannot bring forth sweet and bitter water. So I need to choose. I choose the sweet water. I choose to not live in fear, follow God's instructions, and watch every single word that comes from my mouth. I will think before I say anything to anyone. I will pause reflect then speak. So I know the words coming out of my mouth are edifying; only showing my good character, my peaceful nature, my meekness, and humbled demeanor. Thank you God and I pray you continue to minister to me. In Jesus name Amen!

Printed in the United States
By Bookmasters